Create A New Reality

How to manifest positive change in your life

By

Dwayne Jenkins

Copyright © 2023 Dwayne Jenkins.
All Rights Reserved.
Published by Tritone Publishing

Introduction

This book you now hold in your hand is not about success from a philosophical point of view, but about being successful from a practical application point of view. Meaning that in order to get the most out of it, you will need to take action!

Reading it is fine. It should be a good read. You might even find some of it entertaining. And if that is what you're after, there are plenty of other books to read. But if you are looking to make a change in your life, then this book will do that.

That is if you take the time to learn and understand the lessons presented. That is if you decide to do as instructed and put the lessons into action on a daily basis. And you go through the process it takes to make an everlasting change.

If not, you probably won't get too much out of this book. You might not even finish it. But if you truly have the desire to make a change in your life, and you are willing to do whatever it takes, then you'll get massive value from it.

The lessons presented will give you the guidance and tools necessary to create the life you choose. Whatever that may be. Would you like more money? wouldn't we all? Of course, we would, but for some reason, we all don't have it. How come?

The reason for this is that most people don't want to learn and do what it takes to get it. You see, becoming successful requires a certain type of thinking. Which leads to a certain type of action. Which leads to a certain type of success.

Believe me when I tell you that successful people think and act very differently from unsuccessful people. The rich have a very different point of view about money than the poor and middle class. That is why they are rich and wealthy.

And if you'd like to get rich and become wealthy, then you will need to develop this certain type of thinking that they have as well. And if you're not concerned about money, you should be. For it is the fuel that has gotten you what you have in life now.

So if you are ready to learn how to get more to take your life to the next level, then read on. All I ask is that you follow and do as instructed. If you do, you will achieve things in life you never thought were possible. Are you ready? Then let's go!

Dwayne Jenkins

Table of Contents

Introduction

Chapter 1 Thoughts   1

Think of making change 1
Chapter 1 Summary   7

Chapter 2 Desire 9

Your desire to make that change 9
Chapter 2 Summary   17

Chapter 3 Vision 19

You visualize your new reality 19
Chapter 3 Summary   24

Chapter 4 Emotion   25

Add feeling to your vision   25
Chapter 4 Summary   30

Chapter 5: Faith   31

Believe you can do it   31
Chapter 5 Summary   37

Chapter 6 Strategy 39
Your plan to get there 39
Chapter 6 Summary 45

Chapter 7 Discipline 47
Do whatever it takes 47
Chapter 7 Summary 53

Chapter 8 Affirmations 55
Keep out negativity 55
Chapter 8 Summary 64

Chapter 9 Adversity 65
Lessons within failure 65
Chapter 9 Summary 71

Chapter 10 Expectancy 73
Your order's been received 73
Chapter 10 Summary 77

Chapter 11 Gratitude 79
Show appreciation 79
Chapter 11 Summary 85

Chapter 12 Let It Go 87
Give it time to manifest 87
Chapter 12 Summary 92

Chapter 13 Master Alliance 93
Maximize your potential for success 93
Chapter 10 Summary 98

Create A New Reality Conclusion 99

About The Author 115

Chapter 1 Thought

Think to make a change

Your first step on the journey to independent wealth is the thought of making a change. Making a change from where you are right now, to where you'd like to be somewhere in the future. With hopefully a lot more money.

Thought is the starting point of all achievement. It is where your mind says, "hey, it's time for a change." and so the idea starts to brew in your mind. You start to think that you'd like more out of life. More money than what you have right now.

Maybe you'd like a better vehicle. Or possibly nicer clothes to wear, or have a home of your own to live in. Or if you already have a home, possibly a second one, or a nicer one than the one you are currently living in?

You can have all that and more. You could even build your own financial empire if you'd like. But before you can do any of the above-mentioned, you must first plant the seed of thought in your mind.

Think of your mind as a mental garden. Where you are going to plant seeds of change.

This is what I did. I was working at a regular warehouse job and realized there was no future there. A steady paycheck? Yes. A bright future? Absolutely not! So I thought, I need to make a change. But how?

I didn't want to go get another job with no future, as most jobs are. Plus I knew that I'd never get rich working for someone else. And hopefully, you know this too. And if you don't, you will by the end of this book.

So I thought, and I thought, and I thought. What to do? So you see, all change in anything we do begins with a thought. We see our life from an outside perspective and we realize we need to make a change.

That is why you picked up this book. And possibly many others. Looking for a way to nurture that seed of thought. That thought of change. Well, I can tell you from my own personal experience, this book will show you how to do it.

Of course, you can't just read it. Or any other book like it for that matter. That's not going to do anything. You will have to take action. You will have to feed and water your seed of change in order for it to germinate. Just as I did.

And that is what I am going to teach you in this book. How to manifest positive change by creating a new reality.

The main thing you will need to do is increase your income. Because that is the only way to make a change in any area of life. When you build or change any type of landscape, it takes money. And sometimes, lots of it.

Of course, there is more to it than that. But you will need to learn how to make more money in order to get a nicer vehicle, nicer clothes, and a better living arrangement. And if you think not, you are highly mistaken.

This is why most people fail to make lasting changes. They don't change the way they think about money. Or they don't learn how to manage it, respect it, and put it to good use. They earn it, they spend it, and they move on.

Financially successful people do not do this. In fact, successful people think quite differently about money than unsuccessful people. That is why they are rich. Would you like to be rich? Of course, you would. Who wouldn't?

That is why this book is so valuable. It will teach you that. And if you learn the lessons being taught as I did, you will bring abundance into your life. How much? That's up to you. How well you learn, and how much action you take.

This is where 90% of people who study how to get rich and build wealth fail. They don't take enough action!

And so will you if you choose to do the same. I'm hoping that you won't be like those people. I'm hoping that you will learn the lessons, do as instructed, and make a positive change in your life as your seed of thought has suggested.

Becoming financially successful is a lot of work and won't come overnight. It didn't for me. I had to work at it. I got fed up with my life at the time of making a change and decided to do something about it. You will have to do the same.

Since this was way before the internet was the way it is now, I had to go to the library and get books. Books on success, books on business, and books on personal development. All these helped me to make the change I was looking for.

The lessons presented in this book came from the lessons I learned in those books so many years ago. They taught me to get control of my mind and think for myself. I learned that I was in control of my life and could make the change myself.

This I found to be interesting. Being that the people I worked with did not think like this. At least not the production workers. Maybe management. After all, they were the ones making the money.

But I was never going to get in there no matter how hard I tried. So I had to figure out some other way to get ahead.

So I had to look in a different direction. And since I didn't know anyone who was successful, I turned to the wealth of education, the library. Today, you can turn to the internet and watch videos. But there is still much value in books.

Books allow you to digest information slower. They allow you to learn the lessons at your pace, and they allow you to think about what you are reading and how it will affect your life now and in the future.

As I said a little while ago, your change in life and pursuit of financial success will start with a thought. The thought to do it. The thought to figure out how to do it, and the thought that it is possible. After reading this book, you will know it is.

Remember, your thought is a seed that you plant in the soil. The soil in your mind. You then water and fertilize it. Knowing that it is going to expand and develop in a wonderful way. That is if you do it with faith, expectancy, and understanding.

Thought is the most powerful thing in the universe. Your words are thoughts expressed. If you are in a position of authority, then you already know how your thoughts can cause people to take action.

If not, then you already know how other people's words of thought can make you take action. Like at your job.

Change happens when you work voluntarily, or involuntarily with your subconscious mind. Your conscious mind gives the orders, and your subconscious carries them out. Thus being that you can create the life that you choose.

You think it, you believe it to be so, and then you eventually become it. But it is a process that you need to go through. That is why it is called change. Your reality changes as you go through the process. Very much like a caterpillar to a butterfly.

This all starts with a thought. The thought to make a change. Your thoughts are the main ingredient of your power. And when you mix them with the other ingredients that I am going to teach you in this book, you will be able to create change.

And not just change, but any change you choose to manifest. You will be able to create the new reality that you choose. You will select exactly what you want, you will plant the seed, and if you nourish it properly, it will blossom into something wonderful.

That is if you do as instructed. Just like learning to play the guitar. You have to understand the concepts and techniques that are associated with the instrument. You then need to put them into a daily routine of application.

Once you do that, you can create beautiful music. This is no different. Do you want to make a positive change? Learn how.

Chapter 1 Summary

In this first chapter, you learned about the importance of thought. How it affects everything that comes after it. If you want to make a change, you must think about it first.

First, you learned that thought is the starting point of all change. No matter what that change is. You must first develop the thought of change before you can create it.

Second, you learned that thought is a seed that you plant in your mental soil. And like any other type of seed, you will need to nourish it in order for it to grow properly.

Third, you learned that in order to make a change you will also need to increase your income. This will allow you to acquire better things in your life.

Fourth, you learned that successful people think quite differently about money than unsuccessful people. And you will need to do the same if you truly want to make a change.

Fifth, you learned about the subconscious mind. How the conscious mind gives the orders, and the subconscious mind carries them out.

There is a lot to do with the subconscious mind when it comes to making change. Since everything starts with a thought, and that exists in your mind, you will need to learn how to control it. You will need to learn to harness its power.

That is what this training is about. Learning to harness the power you have deep inside you. This power will assist you in making the changes you desire in your life.

But it won't happen overnight. You might see some small advances, but to truly master the science, it will take time, understanding, and practical application.

Remember what I said about learning to play the guitar? This is the same thing. This is not a book you will just read and say "ok I got it" and then change will happen. If it were that easy, everybody would be living a great life.

No, this is a book that will require you to learn, understand, and take daily action. Do that, and I guarantee you will create a new reality beyond your wildest dreams. Like it has for so many others who have come before you.

Chapter 2 Desire

Your desire to make that change

Now that you have firmly established the thought of change in your mind, it is now time to look at your desire. How much of a desire do you truly have for change?

This is the second step toward creating your new reality. You must have the desire to make a change. That means stepping out of your comfort zone and doing things you've never done before. Not the easiest thing to do.

My change came through teaching people how to play guitar. That is what got me out of my going nowhere day job. I knew how to play guitar, and knew how to play in bands. But teach? I didn't know how to do that.

Well, at least not at first. But over time doing as the books instructed, I got better. I stepped out of my comfort zone and gave it a try. I thought I could do it as I had taken lessons, but the actually doing it part was a bit scary at first.

Talk about fake it till you make it. Can you imagine, I'd advertise and then try to convince people to pay me money to teach them what I knew about the guitar?

Well, I wasn't very good at it at first, but I got better. When I discovered this was my calling I ran with it. I studied, took notes, thought about it, put a plan of action together, and put that plan into action.

You will have to do the same. And it is your desire that will put this all into play. Or it won't. It just depends on how much of a desire you have for a change in your life.

This is why most people fail at making change. They think the thought that they should, but their desire is not enough for them to put a plan together and take action upon it. Or they do, and they quit at the first sign of defeat.

This is why your desire for change is so important. If it is strong enough, you will take the rocky road less traveled and not stop until you get to where your desire leads you. No matter what obstacles you might face during the journey.

Your desire has to be so strong that nothing can break it. Like a fire that burns deep inside you that can't be put out no matter how much water you throw on it. It just won't go out! And you will not quit! Is your desire that strong?

Definitely, something to think about. Because if it's not, you'd better spend your time reading another book. A mystery novel or something. But if it is, read on.

As I said, it will not be easy to make the change you are looking to make. To create the new reality that you desire. But it can be done. It has many, many people and you could be added to the list.

But the desire has to be there. You can sit around and think great thoughts, but if they are not backed by a burning desire for their fruition, they will not germinate and grow into something wonderful.

Like the gardener who wants to grow vegetables. He has to really want to do it. He can't just plant the seeds and walk away. He has to water them, fertilize them and give them plenty of sunlight. Put in some work.

Even after all that, he still has to watch out for weeds and bugs that come around. If he's lucky and has the desire to do as expected, the seeds will germinate and pop out of the ground. Great! Success.

Nope. Not yet. He now needs to tend to the plants and make sure they grow as they're supposed to. His desire has to be strong to keep the plants alive knowing that one day he will harvest the seeds that he has sewn.

In a sense, you are doing the same thing. You are planting seeds in your mental garden and learning how to get them to grow. And only the burning desire for this achievement will allow you to make it happen.

Now the best way to get this desire fueled up is to write it out on a sheet of paper. You could write something like. "I desire to double my income within the next 12 months." This would be a good statement to start with.

A statement like this will get the mental juices flowing. And if you were to read it out loud, which I'll explain more about later in the training, it will get your mind focused on the goal and speed up the process of making it happen.

But for now, it will be a good idea to just write it down. And not just that, write a whole bunch of ideas down. Things you want to change or bring about in your life. Be as specific as possible. This will help get your desire fueled up.

The thing you really want to think about to fuel your desire is your why? Why do you want to make a change? Why do you want to create a new reality? I highly recommend you take some time to think about this.

A strong why will also help fuel your burning desire.

This is a step where a lot of people fail in the training. They don't have a big enough reason for doing it. If the reason is strong enough, the mind will make the body go into action to do something about it.

And if the goal is to break a habit like smoking, drinking, or overeating. You definitely need a strong reason. Or else it just won't happen. You hear about this all the time. People try to quit these things and fail.

The reason is that they do not have a big enough desire to do it. They're reasoning is not strong enough. They know they should, and would like to, but since the desire isn't truly there, they eventually give up.

So in order to accomplish change, you must have that burning desire for its attainment. So in this step of the process, you want to look deep within yourself and really pull out your reason or reasons for going through this process.

When you look deep inside yourself and start to write things out, you create a mirror of yourself that you can look at from an outside perspective. And once you do, you might not like some of the things you find. This might be your reason.

Just start thinking, and writing. It will be really good for you.

The thing I love about making change is that I discovered things about myself I didn't know existed. Like, hidden talents. But I also discovered some things that I didn't realize I was doing or thinking and it gave me the motivation to change.

I begin to focus on the positive things that were good in me. I focused less on the things I wasn't good at and my burning desire headed me in a whole new direction. A direction of the unknown. Was it a bit scary? Yeah, it was.

But I got through it and it made me feel better about myself. The fact that I did something I didn't think I could do. Believe me, when you can do that, it is a great feeling. You start to wonder, what else can I do?

I remember when I first started teaching guitar lessons. I would advertise in the newspaper, showing how long I've been doing it, and someone would call and want me to come to their house. I'd be as professional as possible and say "sure, I'll be there."

Then I'd have to figure out how to get there. And I didn't have GPS or anything, so I'd have to figure it out. Of course, I did, but it was still a bit daunting. I'd then get in my little red truck and head out to their address.

Mind you, these were people of upper financial status, and here I was a local long-haired musician on my way to their house.

I wouldn't know it from the phone call, I'd just go by the address and figure out where to go. But I remember going into their neighborhoods and saying to myself, "I don't belong here." The voice in my head would say "yes you do!"

And so I'd pull up, get out my guitar and walk up to this huge house. Then they'd open the door and say "Hi Dwayne, come on in." I'd walk in and think, I don't belong here. And they'd be so nice to me that I'd forget about that negative thought.

You see, up to this point in my life, I was used to playing loud rock n roll in bars. Dealing with musicians, bar owners, booking agents, and sound engineers. And believe me when I tell you, these are some hard people to deal with sometimes.

That's why the music business is so hard. The jobs are hard, the people are hard, and you have to be a little hard yourself to exist in it. At least this is from my point of view. But then again, that's all I can really teach you from.

Anyway, they would make me feel more than comfortable and allow me to teach them what I knew about the guitar. I basically taught them how I learned. And you know what? It worked. They loved it, paid me, and invited me to come back.

And as of this writing, I'm still doing it almost twenty years later.

And all this could not have been done without a strong desire. A burning one at that. If you truly want to create a new reality in your life, one that will inspire others, you will need that burning desire also.

Look at somebody like Steve Jobs. He had a burning desire to invent a computer for the household person to use. Before he came along, computers existed for business purposes only. No one felt there was a need for one in the home.

Unless you had a home-based business. Which wasn't as popular as it is today. But his computer wasn't for business, although it could be, it was more for pleasure. And it was his burning desire that got that idea off the ground.

When Henry Ford wanted to make cars for the common working man, it hadn't been done before. Sure cars were being made, but for the rich. Not for the working man. Henry Ford set out to change that.

Both he and Steve had a burning desire so strong, that nothing was going to stop them. And this desire goes for many, many other people. Jeff Bezos, Jimmy Page, Jim Hendrix, Milton Hershey, John Lennon, Marilyn Monroe, etc, etc, etc.

Do you see what I'm getting at? Make sure you have that burning desire. If you do, great! If not, then get it!

Chapter 2 Summary

In this second chapter, you have learned about the importance of desire. This is the second step in achieving what you want in life. More money, nicer house, etc.

First, you learned a little bit about my desire and what it helped me to accomplish. I could have never done it without the desire to make a change.

Second, you learned that your desire cannot be half-hearted. It can't be a wish, it has to be a fire that burns deep inside you. It has to be what motivates you to take action.

Third, you learned that you are a mental gardener. You are planting seeds and it is up to you to make them grow. Care for them and eventually harvest what you have sewn.

Fourth, you learned about the importance of writing it down. This is a huge part of the process and should not be overlooked. Write it down and say it out loud.

Fifth, you learned about other people who used their desire to accomplish great things. People like Steve Jobs and Henry Ford. Two people who changed the world.

18

Chapter 3 Vision

You visualize your new reality

Now that you have that burning desire inside you that will not go out no matter what, you can start to focus on your vision. Your vision of the future. How do you see your life once this new reality has manifested?

This is where you get in touch with the second most powerful tool you possess. Your imagination. Everything in the world was created twice. Once in the imagination, and then once in reality.

Take Henry Ford's car for instance. He had to imagine what his car would look like and what it might be capable of doing once he built it. Same with Steve Jobs. He had to imagine what his computer would look like and how it might function.

They also had to visualize what the future would look like. Their future as well as how their inventions would impact other people's futures. And all this is done through the power of the imagination.

You want to take some time to visualize what you want so that your mind gets a clear picture of it.

You want it to be so clear, that you can write it out in full detail. Another writing assignment for you. This is important because it impresses this picture in your subconscious mind. Which will eventually help you to create it.

Remember what I said about the subconscious mind? Your conscious mind gives the orders, and your subconscious mind carries them out. So that's the case. You want to be clear in the orders that you give.

This is one of the things that people get wrong as well when trying to manifest their desires. They don't have a clear enough picture of what they want. So the mind gets confused as to what to deliver.

You must be crystal clear about what you want. In fact, if you can be so clear about your vision that you can see it right now, then you are already on your way to creating it. Now, if you say things like "I'm not good at visualizing," you are wrong.

The reason I say this is because everything you have in your life right now was brought in through visualization. Your vehicle for instance. Unless someone just gave you a vehicle, you thought about what kind you wanted.

You thought, visualized, and with enough desire, went out to get it. And now it is in your life.

So, if you feel you can't visualize, and you want to create a new reality, you are going to have to learn to visualize. Or else go read another book. Like I said in the beginning, this book is about practical application.

These are success principles that must be applied on a daily basis. Just like gardening. You must not read, put the book down and say "I got it." Unless you are going to go take massive action on the ideas presented.

Remember, this is like learning a new language. Your mind is very powerful. Especially your imagination. And if you learn to use it properly, you can create anything that you desire. And I do mean anything.

But once again, it comes down to your desire. Your desire to bring that vision into reality. When you take time to work with your imagination, you can visualize your future as if you were living it right now,

And that my friend is the idea. Imagine what your life would be like if you had your new reality in your life right now. You then start living like it already exists. But in order to do that, you have to have a vision.

Can you visualize your new reality in specific detail? Much like the gardener can visualize his crops.

If you are a mental gardener, which you are, then you must visualize how beautiful the garden will look when everything has grown and is ready to be harvested. You must be able to see the tomato plant in all its glory.

Henry Ford said he wanted to see people going places in his vehicles. He wanted people in the city to be able to go out to the country, and people out there to visit family and friends in the city.

That was his vision. And sure enough, he made that happen. Steve Jobs was the same way. He wanted to invent the computer for the school teacher, garbage man, janitor, or artist. And sure enough, he did.

These two men and many others had a vision. They could clearly see in their mind what they wanted to create, and their minds helped them to bring it into reality. Your mind will do the same thing. But you have to have a vision.

Once you have this vision you must write it out in clear detail and hold steady with it. Hold it in your mind. See it so clearly that you have it in your reality right now today. If it's a new car you want, imagine you are driving it right now.

If it is a new home, imagine you are living in it right now. Whatever your hearts desire, vision it as already here.

What this does, is trick the subconscious mind into believing that it is so. When you do this, it begins to act in a certain way. Kind of like training a pet with a treat. You condition them to act a certain way through positive reinforcement.

All successful people have a vision for their objectives. So you must too. And like I said, you need to be able to write it out in specific detail. Just like you did with the other things I taught you.

This is what I did. I wrote out what I wanted to accomplish. I wrote out that I saw myself teaching people in their homes. When I'd drive to the store, I'd go into a neighborhood and act as if I was going to teach someone in that neighborhood.

I'd drive by these really nice homes and imagine that I was going inside and teaching them or their kids how to play guitar. That was my vision. I would imagine when I was on break at work. Imagine that I was getting paid to teach.

And before you know it, I'd get a call from someone wanting me to come to their home and teach them. Then I'd be on my way to go teach in one of those types of homes I was envisioning. I'd go inside, teach, get paid, and be on my way.

That's how it works. You create your vision, hold it steady, and act as if you already have it. Then it will manifest.

Chapter 3 summary

In chapter three you learned about having a vision. A vision of what exactly it is you want to accomplish. This will help you to stay focused on your objective.

<u>First</u>, you learned that all successful people have a clear concise vision of what they want. You must too. This is part of why most people fail. Lack of vision.

<u>Second,</u> you learned about the power of your imagination. This is where your new reality will start. You create it twice. Once in your mind, then once in reality.

<u>Third</u>, you learned about the importance of writing it out on a piece of paper in specific detail. The more detailed the better. This helps to send the message to the subconscious mind.

<u>Fourth</u>, you learned a bit more about my experience and what I did with my vision. How I envisioned certain things and they eventually came to pass.

<u>Fifth,</u> you learned about how acting as if you have your new reality right now is highly important. Very much like training a pet with reinforcement.

Make sure you have a vision of your objective!

Chapter 4 Emotion

Add feeling to your vision

Now that you have a vision, you want to bring that vision to life. You do this by adding feeling to your vision. This kind of goes with what I was saying in the last chapter. About how you imagine it's already here.

When you add feeling and emotion to your vision it cements it in the subconscious mind. It lets the mind know that you are serious about bringing this to fruition and it needs to carry out this order.

It is the feeling and emotion that you tie to your vision that will make this so. Remember the training your pet analogy I mentioned earlier? Well, if you've ever done that, you know it's when you add feeling and emotion to it that makes it work.

If you give an order to a dog for the first time, it doesn't obey. It's only adding feeling and emotion to the command that makes all the difference. You envision your dog acting a certain way. Lying down, rolling over, etc.

And after adding feeling and emotion to this command the dog eventually hears you and does it.

Your subconscious mind works very much the same way. You have to get its attention and train it to do what you want it to. And since everyone's desires are different it's hard to know what method works the best.

But we do know, that adding feeling and emotion to the vision you have for yourself will move you in the right direction. This has been proven time, and time again. That is why it is so important to write it out and get a clear picture.

This helps to train the mind that this is what you want to create. Kind of like a blueprint of a home. When a home is built, they don't just start putting materials together. They create a blueprint and build the house accordingly.

And when action is taken on that blueprint with emotion and feeling, the home starts to be created into physical reality. And since there is a clear concise vision of what it should look like, it makes it easier to build.

Your vision of what you want to create should be no different. If you want to double your income within the next twelve months, you need to see clearly how you're going to do that. You must give in order to receive.

That is not my law, it is the law of the universe. To receive, one must give in an equal amount. So think of this as well.

Adding feeling to your vision will allow you to create a greater impact on the success and abundance you are attracting. When you can actually feel your vision, you will make it manifest more quickly.

The reason for this is that your feelings allow you to raise your vibrations. You attract into your life through vibrations. This is because everything in the universe is made up of energy. And all energy vibrates.

So by adding feeling and emotion to your vision, you get excited about it. You get motivated to do what is necessary to make it happen.

And when it begins to start developing like the planted seed I mentioned earlier, you will get excited about making that seed grow. You will have fun nurturing it. Watering it, fertilizing it, giving it sunlight, and taking care of it.

But this can only be done through feeling and emotion. Like the old saying, "I'm living the dream." Well, when you get excited about your vision, you will be living the dream. That's what I did when I started getting paid to teach guitar lessons.

Which by the way, was a lot more than I was getting paid to play in a band.

I got excited! I added feeling and emotion to my vision, and I started to get a steady stream of paying clients. Now of course, this didn't come overnight, but it did start to manifest once I added the other ingredients to the stew of success.

Success in what you want is like baking bread. You have to have all the ingredients working together in unison for it to rise when you put it in the oven. If not, it won't come out right. So make sure you learn all the steps in this book.

When you put feeling into your vision, not only will it help you to get closer to your objective, but it will also tell the universe that you deserve to be successful. You deserve it because you are willing to do as instructed.

Remember, this is an action guidebook. It gives you the principles necessary to make the change you are looking to make. But you have to be willing to give in return for them. There is nothing for free in the world of success.

If you want to double your income as I mentioned earlier, you have to see it in your vision and put feeling and emotion into it. That way you will double your income. That is if you do everything else that is taught in this book.

You must follow through with everything that is in the training. Never forget that. It is vitally important.

Once you start to really feel your vision, you will see things change within you. You will be more excited, you will have more energy, and you will be ready to go. Like an athlete pumped to win a game.

This will help keep you in a positive state of mind. If you do this every day it will bring more joy into your life. More happiness, and the feeling of expectancy, knowing that you are on your way to attracting great opportunities.

And it is these surprise opportunities that are going to allow you to manifest what you desire. Remember, you receive more of what you are broadcasting out to the universe. Feeling that your new reality is here, it'll help bring it to you faster.

The reason for this is because of your vibrational energy. Vibrations seek out other vibrations that they are in harmony with. This is how music works. All instruments need to be tuned to the same vibrational frequency.

When they are, they sound good. Great even. But if one instrument is out of vibrational alignment, it sounds bad. You are doing the same thing. Getting in tune with the vibration of what you desire.

Add feeling and emotion to your vision, and before you know it, you will be living your new reality.

Chapter 4 Summary

In chapter 4 you have learned that to bring your vision to life, you must add feeling and emotion to it. This will help you to keep it steady in your mind.

First, you learned that it helps to train your subconscious to carry out the order that you have instructed it to do. Help you to create your new reality.

Second, you learned that your vision is a blueprint that when equipped with feelings of emotion will help you manifest it faster into your life.

Third, you learned that adding feeling to your vision raises your vibration. And it is this raise in vibration that will attract the opportunities necessary to bring this about.

Fourth, you learned that adding feeling and emotion to your vision will make you feel better about yourself. Get you excited, and help you to learn all the other steps necessary.

Fifth, you learned that when you raise your vibration by adding emotion to your vision, you get in vibrational harmony with the frequency that your desire exists on.

Always add emotion to your vision and it will manifest faster.

Chapter 5 Faith

Believe you can do it

Now that you are starting to get your mental motor running, it is time to talk about faith. Faith is the belief that you can do it. This is a must-have tool that belongs in your successful toolbox. If you don't have it, you'll need to get it.

The reason for this is that like I said before, creating change is not easy. You see people fail at this all the time. You might have even in the past. I know I have many times. So has all successful people.

And being that's the case, there is no need to worry. Because if you develop faith, nothing can stop you from accomplishing your dream. It's kind of like that burning desire I talked about earlier. Your faith must be that strong too.

On your journey to your new reality, you will run into obstacles, setbacks, and unpleasantries. Nothing can be done about it. It is all part of the process. But with unshakeable faith, you will figure out a way to get through them.

Faith has a lot of power to it itself. In fact, just having faith and the willpower to do it would probably be enough.

But if you have all the steps in this book working together in harmony, you will definitely create your new reality. And be able to do it with style. But for now, let's focus on the power of faith and the fact that it is absolutely necessary to have.

When Henry Ford decided to make a different kind of automobile than what was currently being made, a lot of people opposed his idea. Especially wealthy investors. They didn't think it was a good idea. So they wouldn't invest.

Same thing with Steve Jobs. When he wanted to create a computer for the everyday person, he ran into the same problem. Nobody thought anyone would buy a computer for anything other than business.

But both of these men had to have faith. Faith that they would find the right people to invest in their ideas. Faith in themselves that once they did, they could actually make it work. Henry Ford ran into all kinds of problems when he first started.

So much, so that investors pulled their funding. Thus making him have to figure out how to correct the problems so that he could start again with some new investors. It took a whole lot of faith to be able to do that.

When you head down the road to your personal success, beware of opposing ideas. Believe me, they'll be there.

This is where your faith will come in. If you happen to mention your ideas to the wrong person, they might try to bring you down with their negative thinking. They might even try to talk you out of the idea. Make you feel it's not possible.

If and when this happens, what do you think will pull you through? Faith! That's what will pull you through. When you try things and they don't work out, what will keep you pressing forward? Faith!

Remember the mental garden I talked about? What happens to gardens as they blossom? Weeds pop up and bugs come in. They come in and try to take over your garden. And if you not careful, they will.

That is why having faith is so important. Your bugs and weeds will come in the form of negative thoughts. Negative thoughts from inside your mind, and from outside people. And if you are not careful, these thoughts will take over your mental garden.

When those pesky negative thoughts come around, you have to spray them with weed killer. This is faith. When you get opposing thoughts of "you can't do it", or "you'll fail", it is faith that will keep them at bay.

And the more your head down the road, the more they will try to derail your progress.

Look at the Super Bowl between the Atlanta Falcons and the New England Patriots. Through three-quarters of the game, the Atlanta Falcons dominated. They scored and kept New England from scoring.

By half-time, it was a no-brainer who was going to win this one. In fact, it was so obvious that people started to leave the game. By the third quarter, Altlanta had a 28-3 lead over New England. The victory parties were already starting.

Then, something strange happened. Something that has never happened in Super Bowl history. The Patriots began to get their game on. The defense started making stops and the Patriot's offense started to score points.

Now surely they couldn't expect to win by now. I mean, after all, the game was almost three-quarters over. But because New England held faith in themselves, they came back to tie the game and go into overtime.

And not only that, but they actually won the game. To come back and win from a 28-3 deficit could only happen through the power of faith. The chips were down, but they didn't waver. They kept pushing until they won.

It was faith in themselves that they could win that allowed this to happen. You must have this faith in yourself too.

When you believe in yourself to the point you know you can do it, you create strength of willpower. The power of commitment to the end result. Just like the Patriots in that game. You develop relentless persistence and uncommon discipline.

You will stay on the path for the duration of the journey, and you will do whatever it takes to manifest your desire. Remember, what you learned about your desire? Faith will help add fuel to the fire and keep it burning.

Faith will not only give you the strength to get started but give you the strength to keep going. This is the hard part. Many people get started down the road of their own personal success, but very few see it to the end.

One of the reasons is that they don't have enough faith in themselves. Deep down they don't truly feel they can do it. So they quit before they get to their wonderful new paradise. This is why having faith to persist is so special.

You get into a very special club that very few are ever permitted into. Only the ones who develop faith and stay the course until the end can enter the special club. The club of winners. The ones who held faith through thick and thin.

I say develop faith because that is what needs to be done. And only through the actions of previous chapters is this possible.

Another thing that faith and belief in yourself does is it creates resilience. This is the ability to bounce back from adversity. To get back on the horse after you have gotten knocked off. You won't survive adversity, you'll get stronger because of it.

And when you run into adversity, which no doubt you will. Faith will allow you to learn from it and try again with new insights. A new plan of action. A new way of looking at things.

So in a sense, you could say that these setbacks you will encounter will be necessary. If looked at from the right point of view. This is another reason people fail. They don't learn the lessons taught in adversity. Successful people always do.

So if you look at it from a positive point of view, you could say they are tests. Tests to see if you really deserve to create a new reality. Especially the kind of reality that is full of wealth and abundance.

Faith will also improve your focus. Elite performers always carry an unwavering focus on what needs to be done. Whether it is a certain task, the next step, or a lesson needing to be learned from adversity. Faith helps them to do this.

And so it will you as well. And as you go through the training, your faith will become stronger, and you more confident.

Chapter 5 Summary

In this chapter, you learned about the power of faith, and that it is a must to develop. For it is what will pull you through tough times and allow you to believe in yourself.

First, you learned that faith is a tool that can really help you to protect your dream. Protect your mental garden. Protect your garden from pesky negative weeds and bugs.

Second, you learned that along your journey, you will encounter opposing ideas. Just like Henry Ford and Steve Jobs. And it is faith that will give you the will to block them out.

Third, you learned about the Patriots winning the Super Bowl against Atlanta. A remarkable feat that was history in the making. All done by the power of faith.

Fourth, you learned how faith helps to develop other skills within you. Discipline, willpower, and confidence. These are all needed to succeed on your journey to your new reality.

Fifth, you learned how faith will help you to get through adversity. And that there are lessons to be learned. And learning them will give you the edge needed.

Remember, there are hidden gems in failure. Find them.

Chapter 6 Strategy

Your plan to get there

Now is the time to think about your plan of action. Your strategy of how you are going to get to where you are going. This will be a plan that helps guide your decisions and use of resources effectively.

Your strategy will outline your plan to achieve your vision. A how-to on what you are willing to give for that which you desire. Remember I talked about this earlier in the training? How you have to give in order to get.

Now, you want to look at what you wrote down and think about how you are going to accomplish creating it. Creating your new reality. Anything that has been created starts with a vision. Once that is created, it is time for its achievement.

This is why I wanted you to put as much emotion into it as possible. That way you have a clear picture of what you want to create. Now you just have to figure out how to do it. What are the steps necessary to bring it to life?

This is where you will give all that you have. This is where you will let the universe know you are worthy of your desire.

The reason I say this is because that is what it is going to take. If your vision is big, it will take big thinking to bring it to fruition. Just like the gardener analogy, if you want one plant, it takes so much work to produce.

But if you want more, that will take extended effort. Possibly more planning. And maybe even more steps to get it to manifest as you see in your vision. Can you see how all these steps work upon each other?

It is very much like learning to play rhythm on the guitar. You first start by learning to form chords. Then you learn to switch between them. Then you put a few together to form a chord progression. Then you learn to strum the chords in a certain time sequence to create rhythm.

And it has to be in that order or else it won't work. You can learn to play individual chords, but if you can't switch between them, you can't create rhythm. If you can strum but can't form the chords, you can't create rhythm.

This works the same exact way. As I said in the beginning it starts with a thought. Then desire, vision & emotion. Once you have that, then you can plan your action. But planning action without desire won't do you any good.

This is why a lot of people fail at creating the life they want.

Now that you have an understanding of what you want and you can see very clearly what it will look like once you receive it, you now need to figure out how to create it. What is the plan of action? Your strategy. Your willingness to give.

Once you have that all figured out, the question is, "where do I start?" well, you start by looking inside your mind and listening to your subconscious. It will give you the plan you need, and once it does, get after it immediately.

Once you have made the decision that you will do whatever it takes, and your subconscious mind believes through your power of faith that you are true to your word, It will start to spit out a plan of action for you.

You will start to think of new ideas that you hadn't thought of before. Or, you'll think of old ideas with a new twist to them. And when this happens, you write it down. Write the ideas down and think about them.

See if you can get to where you write down at least five great ideas that come to you. Ten would be better, but five will be a good start. This training of your mind requires a lot of thought, visualizing, writing, and saying the words.

The more you do this, the faster the mind will let you know what to do. How to create your new reality.

For instance, when I was working on making the change from my going-nowhere job and started teaching, I would think about what to do next. How to go about developing this guitar-teaching business?

After all, I didn't know anything about business. But my mind did. It told me to get books and study. It told me to get books on personal development. Get books on marketing. And get lesson plans ready for when calls would come in.

It told me to think, study, write, say affirmations out loud, meditate on what I wanted, and take action on a daily basis. So I did. I did all that the books said to do, and this fueled my desire to create a new reality.

Let's take the goal I mentioned earlier. The goal or desire to double your income in the next 12 months. Is this possible? Well, it is if you believe it to be. It is if you are willing to do as instructed.

It is if you are willing to hold steady to your purpose. It is if you are willing to keep that fire of burning desire lit within you. But most of all, it is if you are willing to give everything you got to make it happen.

Look at Henry Ford, Steve Jobs, and Jeff Bezos. All were willing to do whatever it took to manifest their ideas.

What are you willing to do? I suggest you get out a piece of paper and write at the top what you want to create. Let's say for sake of argument, you want to double your income. Great idea. A great creation. Write that at the top.

Then divide the paper into two columns. On the top of one column, write things that can bring in more money. In the other column, write down what you are going to have to do in order to make that happen.

Can you see what this does? On one side you are writing down ideas that will bring you more income. And on the side, you are writing down what you will need to do to get that money flowing to you.

This is just an example of doubling your income, but it could be anything that you desire. But I will tell you this, if it is anything materialistic that you desire, a car, house, etc, you will need to increase your income.

So make sure you are always aware of this. And if you want more money to come into your life, you must have a positive attitude towards it. Never feel bad about money. It is a positive energy that has done a lot of good.

And the only bad it has ever appeared to do was from the people who handled it.

Remember, it is no good or bad with money. It is what people do with it that makes it so. Money is only a means of exchange. But it does have a certain energy to it. And it flows to those who attract it into their lives.

What people do with it is a whole different story. But as I told you in the very beginning, it starts with a thought. Many people think about wanting a better life, they know the money will get it for them, so they pursue it.

Either they put in extra hours at their job, or exchange something material for its value. There are really only two honest ways to get money. Work, save, or borrow. Gambling is a way as well, but you have to first come up with the money.

Same thing with investing. You have to somehow come up with the money to invest to make more money. Now if you can create something to sell out of what you already have, then that's a way to make money different than mentioned above.

But you still have to of came up with the money for the materials at one time in your life. The point that I am making, is that you want to be honest with acquiring money. Sure you can steal it, but that is not honest.

Get your strategy figured out. Listen to your mind for steps to take, write them out, and then start advancing forward.

Chapter 6 Summary

In this chapter, you have learned about creating a strategy of action for your vision's achievement. All great ideas big or small have a plan of action for their creation.

First, you learned that this is where you will give for what you want to receive. Remember, there are no free rides. All must be paid in one way or another.

Second, you learned that all steps in the training are necessary to have. So make sure you do. If not, go back and get them. It will make all the difference.

Third, you learned that your subconscious mind will give you the steps of your strategy. But in order for it to do that, it must truly believe you are going to do what it takes to carry it out.

Fourth, you learned the importance of writing out these steps once they are given to you. This helps to reinforce them in your mind, which will direct your body to move forward.

Fifth, you learned that money is not good or bad, but just is. A means of exchange that has energy. And it will flow to those who work to attract it. But be honest with it when you get it.

Develop your plan of action and get moving on it at once!

46

Chapter 7 Discipline

Do whatever it takes

The next step of importance to creating your new reality is discipline. Once you get moving forward on your battle plan, you must develop the discipline to keep at it. This is another reason why people fail.

They lack the discipline to keep going. Some don't even get started. In fact, a certain percentage will only read this book and never take action on the instructions presented. Then they'll say "that stuff doesn't work."

Well, as they say in A.A., It works if you work it. That is how this training works. It will work for you if you are willing to work for it. An equal means of exchange. Just like anything else in your life.

The problem is, that most people want something for nothing. I see this all the time with people wanting to make money on the internet. They want to be able to do everything for free. All the tools they use they want to be free.

Is wanting free tools to use to make money an equal exchange? Somebody had to create those tools. Don't they need to be compensated?

I mean, after all, the people using the tools want to be paid for using them. And of course, they eventually will if they have the discipline to see it through. See, discipline is a huge part of your success in creating anything new in your life.

You can have the vision and the strategy you're going to take for its achievement. And you can even start moving forward on its development, but if you don't have the discipline to see it through, it will not manifest into reality.

To make any strategy work in the long run, you must have discipline. So, what is discipline? It is the bridge you need to cross that lies between your plan and your end result. Your new creation.

This is really what has gotten the most successful people to create great things in their lives. They crossed that discipline bridge. They did daily whatever it took to get there. They didn't let anything stop them.

When they ran into a roadblock, they found a way to get over it, through it, or around it. It is the discipline that allowed them to do it. And so it will be the same for you. You will be required to do the same on your journey.

Creating your new reality will be a journey you take. And there will be setbacks. Discipline will allow you to overcome them.

Think about what you want now, and what you want most. That is discipline. The ability to do what you need to do when you need to do it. At a time when you don't feel like doing it. This is where most people fail.

It is easy to do something when you feel like doing it. But it is hard to do something when you don't feel like doing it. It is the discipline that is the difference between the two. It is this discipline that creates casualties.

People think that it is easy to manifest a new reality. To make a change, to create something artistically wonderful. But nothing could be further from the truth. In my experience of creating one for myself, I can tell you, it is a lot of hard work.

And not only that, it is a lot of hard work on a daily consistent basis. That is why only about two percent of the entire population is rich. Because they have the discipline to keep going even when they don't feel like it.

Can you do that? This is where your commitment to your purpose and your burning desire will be tested. To see if they are strong enough. Do you have the willpower to press forward when you don't feel like it?

Remember adding emotion to your vision? Well, discipline will test that emotion.

It is in doing that which you don't feel like doing, that will move your life on the fast track. The track where few run on. The track where people who truly want to make a change will exist until their desire comes to fruition.

This ability to get things done no matter how you feel will help you to focus. Will help you to feel good about yourself. This is why it is important to keep your desires a secret. Because most people aren't that disciplined.

So they may think it strange what you are doing. Getting up at 5:30 in the morning to go jog, staying up late to write things out, or meditate on ideas. Or that you're studying how to work with the subconscious mind, for a great plan of action.

Or that you are working day and night to change the life you have, to the life you want. It takes discipline to do all this. And only those who practice it on a daily basis will get to where they are going.

The great thing about discipline is that practicing it will make you feel better about yourself. So it will develop new skillsets. You'll be more aware, more confident, and more assured. This will allow you to rise above the crowd.

Which is where you'll need to be to create change.

The reason why discipline is so hard for most people is that it takes you out of your comfort zone. And that can be a bit scary. It is like going into the cave you fear to enter to find the treasure you seek.

In fact, that is exactly how it is. How many people do you think to want to do that? Well, a lot of people want to, but how many actually do? The successful ones. That's who. So, the question is, will that be you?

Will you master discipline so that you can be one of the few that enter the cave of fear to get the treasure you seek? Well, you better be. Or else all the work you have done so far will be for nothing. You have been doing as instructed correctly?

I hope you're not just reading this book and saying "yeah, I'll do it later." Because if you are, I'll say "I appreciate you reading it, but that alone won't allow you to create your new reality, and you'd be better of to read a romance novel or something."

As I said in the very beginning, this is a book of practical application. If you have forgotten that, I suggest you go back and read it again. Read it until it is etched in your brain. As I stated before, this is the reason for most people's failure.

Most people don't think it can actually work, so they don't take action. If you know it to be true, then let's continue.

Remember I talked about belief? Not only must you believe in yourself and what you are capable of, but you must also believe without a doubt that these principles work and they are going to help you to create your new reality. And everything in it.

And it will take a whole lot of everything in this writing working in harmony like an engine, to make it so. That is why discipline is so important. Along with everything else. Thinking, visualizing, writing, desire, emotion, strategy, and discipline.

All this and more will be needed by you to accomplish what you have that fire inside you lit for. And if you do as instructed, and be part of the very few, you will be qualified to enter into that special club.

That special club of people who thought it, believed it, and did whatever it took to be it. Would you like that? I hope so. That is why I'm spending time writing this book. To help you achieve the opportunity to get into this special club.

But in order to do this, you must have discipline. You must have the discipline to do whatever it takes to create your new reality. That is why all the other things presented in the previous chapters are so important.

This will present new doors of opportunity that you can open, and walk into a whole new world of possibility.

Chapter 7 Summary

In the seventh chapter, you have learned about discipline. This will be the bridge between where you are, and where you want to be. A bridge you will need to cross.

First, you learned that most people fail at manifesting their new reality because they lack the discipline to stick with it until it happens. Discipline is a must for you, and don't forget it.

Second, you learned how discipline is needed to help overcome setbacks. It is only through discipline that you will be able to get over and through roadblocks.

Third, you learned that discipline is what makes you do what needs to be done when you don't feel like it. This is what separates the winners from the losers.

Fourth, you learned that discipline is what will separate you from the crowd. The reason for this is that it is what will allow you to step out of your comfort zone.

Fifth, you learned that discipline will also allow you to enter a very special club. The club where people exist on the road less traveled to accomplish their dreams.

54

Chapter 8: Affirmations

Keep out negativity

As I mentioned before, on your journey to creating your new reality, whatever that may be, you are going to encounter negativity. Negative thoughts from your mind, as well as from outside sources.

Mainly people. People who have tried to do what you are doing and failed. Or better yet, haven't even tried once. And your mind, which is full of negative thought patterns that will try to creep in and derail your progress.

Why would your mind do this you ask? Well, it's because we have two sides to life. The left and the right. Up and down, in and out, and positive and negative. This is what gives life balance. Ever seen a coin with only one side printed?

How about a dollar bill? Could we have a day without a night? Not likely. Same thing with thoughts. We have positive as well as negative. And it is this positive thought that you want to master to manifest your desires.

You want to master positive thoughts while keeping out the negative ones. Not an easy thing to do on a daily basis.

But it can be done through affirmations. What are affirmations you ask? Well, they are positive sayings that you repeat daily to keep you in a positive mindset. Think of them like mental weed killers.

Do you remember what I said about the mental garden? Well, these affirmations will help to keep out the weeds and bugs, Which will come in the form of negative thinking. And they will come from every angle.

Have you ever seen the movie The Road Warrior with Mel Gibson? Well, it's a movie about how fuel is the bloodline for life. And every time a car comes roaring down the highway, scavengers from all over come to attack it.

They do this for fuel. Because in the movie, which is set in the future, fuel is life. So it has to be protected from all these scavengers. Very much the same way animals in nature have to protect their food.

Have you ever watched a nature program about lions and hyenas? It's quite interesting. The lions make a kill to feed their family, and once they do, here come the hyenas. Ready to take it from them.

So the lions have to protect their food. The cheetahs have it worse because they can't protect it. So they have to let it go.

Think of these negative thoughts like the hyenas or scavengers in the movie I just mentioned. You have to protect your dream. And when thoughts of all kinds find out you are heading down the path of positivity, look out!

This is where affirmations come in. They help to seal up the doors and windows in the winter so that cold air doesn't enter. And you know how the winter cold air is, it will try to come in at any chance it gets.

So you must keep it out. The positivity in your mind needs to keep out the negativity, and this is done with affirmations. This will also help to keep you focused and fuel your journey to a positive change in your life.

In addition to that, it will help you with your subconscious mind. Remember I told you about the importance of this in creating your new reality? The subconscious mind is a very important tool to have, and you must master how to use it.

All successful people harness the power of their subconscious mind to help the attainment of their desire. And in doing so, they reach heights of great proportion. You too will need to do the same.

Affirmations will help to set new positive thought patterns in your subconscious mind and keep you moving forward.

This is a must. You start by reading your desire out loud at least twice daily. Once when you wake up, and once before going to bed. When you wake up your mind is fresh from sleep, so this is a good time to install the affirmation.

When you say it aloud before you go to bed, this hands it over to your subconscious mind to figure out how to make it happen. Remember, your subconscious works 24/7. It is what keeps your heart beating while you sleep.

It's what keeps you breathing. Blood flows through your body and so forth. Since it is always active until you die, it can be a very valuable resource for figuring out how to do things. Like, how to create your greatest triumph.

Affirmations are how you communicate with them. Remember I said to act as if what you want is in your life now? Well, affirmations help to do this. They help you to train your mind to manifest your deepest desires.

Affirmations also help you to stay focused on why you are doing what you are doing on a daily basis. They build confidence and help to rewire your mind for success. Like I said in the very beginning, Successful people think a certain way.

So here are some affirmations that I recommend you use for all the reasons I have mentioned. It is a vital part of the training.

"I am a magnet for money and it is flowing in my direction right now as I speak."

"Prosperity of every kind is drawn to me wherever it is that I work, and I am deeply appreciated and well compensated."

"I live in a loving abundant harmonious universe and I am grateful every day for what I have right now."

"I am now willing to be open to the unlimited prosperity that is all around me."

"Life supplies all my needs in great abundance, and for this, I trust life and feel good about living each day."

"I believe in the law of attraction and in doing so, it brings abundance and prosperity into my life on a daily basis."

"I am so happy and grateful that money comes to me on a daily basis in increasing quantities on a continuous basis."

"I move from poverty thinking to prosperity thinking and my finances are a reflection of this change."

"I express gratitude for all the good in my life and each day brings wonderful new surprises."

"I deserve the best and I accept the best now that I have released all resistance to money. In doing so, I allow it to flow joyously into my life."

"All the good in my life comes from everywhere and everyone and I feel grateful for the abundance that it is bringing my way."

"Negative thoughts go away. You will not ruin my positivity today. I banish you now, forever and you will abide by my ruling."

"The universe is full of abundance and there is no need to worry that I will not receive my share. All I need to do is believe, and it is mine."

"When I ask and believe, the universe answers and delivers what I want without question. It is on its way to me right now and I feel happy for its attainment."

"I am a wonderful person who wants to not only help myself but others as well. This is why the universe picks me to be abundant wealthy and rich."

"Since I have the power to change my mind, I also have the power to change my life. And feel grateful that the power of the universe will help me to do this."

Practice saying these every day without hesitation. Say them out loud with feeling. Remember what I said about adding emotion and feeling to your vision. Well here is another reason for doing that.

This is another place where people fail. They think it's stupid to say these things out loud because it is not part of our everyday routine of life. But to successful people everywhere it is. Look at athletes for example.

They are always getting pumped up before the game with positive affirmations. Winning at anything is as much mental as it is physical. More so, because the body always follows the mind.

There is a saying I read in a book once, I believe it was the book Think and Grow Rich, that said something like "The battle isn't always won by the stronger or faster man, but eventually won by the one who thinks he can."

Meaning that you must think of yourself as a winner in order to do so. Affirmations help you to accomplish this. Notice the wording in some of these I have presented. They talk about life, money, the universe, and gratitude.

All the things needed to succeed at creating your new reality. And like I said before, it is not an easy path to travel.

These affirmations and many more that you will come across on your journey will be like a shield that will help to protect you from the elements within the storm. Affirmations are a very powerful tool so be sure to use them daily.

I recommend you say them as you look in the mirror so you can see your reaction as you say them. But if you feel weird about that, then just say them out loud once when you wake up, and once before going to bed.

Throughout the day would also help. As many times as possible. Create a vision board of what you want your new reality to look like and say these affirmations as you look at it. Add feeling and emotion.

This is a must if you want the aid of your subconscious mind to help manifest what you desire. This is the way to activate it and train it to work for you like the best assistant you could ever have. The best friend or partner.

But in order to do so, you must give it specific instructions of what you want and believe it to be possible for it to believe it too. Then it will work day and night to figure out a way to make it a reality.

Never underestimate the power of your subconscious mind and the affirmations that help to activate and communicate with it.

The assembly line that Henry Ford invented changed the automobile industry. How do you think he figured out how to do it? The subconscious mind. He invented the V8 engine which made a huge impact on the auto industry. How did he do it?

By communicating with his subconscious mind. What about Steve Jobs and the iPhone? How about Thomas Edison and the light bulb? All creations came through the power of the subconscious mind.

Affirmations are the doorway to its use. To make it believe that you are worthy of what you are shooting for and that you can have anything you desire. And it is its job to help you get it. So take this lesson seriously and use these affirmations.

Use them as intended to keep out negativity, stay positive, to communicate with the subconscious mind, keep the faith, stay disciplined, and keep your purpose steady. All this will be needed for you to create your new wonderful reality.

And if you do as instructed as I hope you do, you will begin to see, very slowly at first, a shift in consciousness. A different mindset will begin to develop. You'll begin to see the world from a whole new perspective.

Affirmations will get your mind programmed for success. And once it is, there will be no stopping you! The sky's the limit!

Chapter 8 Summary

In this chapter, you have learned about affirmations. A powerful tool used by all successful people. To be effective, they must be repeated on a daily basis out loud!

<u>First</u>, you learned that affirmations help to keep out negativity. Thoughts of negativity will be all around you and you must keep them at bay at all times.

<u>Second</u>, you learned that affirmations are like mental weed killers. If you are a mental gardener, then you will need these to keep out the weeds and bugs that try to take over.

<u>Third</u>, you learned That affirmations are what is needed for you to reprogram your subconscious mind. To activate it and put it to work assisting you in your quest for a new reality.

<u>Fourth</u>, you learned that Henry Ford and others like him used their subconscious mind to come up with great ideas that changed the world. You too can do the same.

<u>Fifth</u>, you learned that affirmations will help build confidence and self-assurance, and keep you on track to attaining that which you desire. Repeat them out loud as often as possible.

Do not overlook the power of affirmations!

Chapter 9: Adversity

Lessons within failure

Another thing that I have learned in studying successful people, is that they always learn from their failures. Now to most people, failure is when you stop and give up. But not to those who pursue success.

Nope, they welcome failure. The reason why is that they know that there are lessons to be learned from failure. Not to mention the fact that they are determined to accomplish their goals no matter what.

Remember what you learned about discipline? Well, those of success, know it too well. Meaning they are not willing to let any failure or adversity stop them from manifesting what they desire.

And so you must be this way too. When you get knocked off the horse, you must brush yourself off, get back on and keep going. You must have such a definite purpose of why you want to create your new reality, that this does not phase you.

That is the way of successful people. This is why your mind has to be trained to think a certain way.

When Henry Ford set out ot make vehicles for the working man, which had never been done up to that point, he had to figure out a way to bring the cost down per car. And in doing so, he went through many failures.

When Thomas Edison was attempting to invent the light bulb, it is said he failed about ten thousand times before he got it right. Can you imagine that? Attempting to do something over ten thousand times to get it right?

Most people would stop after ten times. Let alone ten thousand times. But that is the way of creation. You must fail in order to figure out what works. Especially when you try to create something that does not exist yet.

When he was asked if he felt like a failure after so many attempts, he said "no, I just figured out another way of not how to do it." Can you see how his thinking was coming from a certain perspective?

He did this because he knew there were lessons to be learned from every failure. And to him, it wasn't failure it was an educated lesson. A lesson to be learned about how to do it better. Or where the boundaries were.

The boundaries of what worked and what didn't. And it was his purpose and burning desire that kept him going.

Same thing when Henry Ford invented the V8 engine. It has been said that for every success, there were over a hundred failures. Did those failures stop him? No! They taught him a lesson. They taught him how not to do it.

When the Wright Bros were attempting to invent flight, they also went through many failures. They had to, being that nobody knew how to fly yet. Many people were trying it at the time but hadn't figured it out.

The Wright Bros would create a glider, get it up in the air, it would crash, break, and they'd have to go back to the hanger and fix it. Then they'd have to figure out what went wrong and try again.

You too will have this kind of adversity with what you are trying to create in your new reality. And like these people, you must not think of failure, but lessons to be learned. I know from past experience, that I have failed many, many times.

And believe me, each one was a learning experience. As most failures in life are. See, we all fail. It's how we look at those failures and what we choose to do about them that makes all the difference.

It is what separates the rich from the poor and middle class.

You see this happen in sports. The team gets on the field and executes a strategy to win. They then find out what works and what doesn't. If something is working, they try it again. You see this in baseball all the time.

The pitcher throws a fastball, and the hitter misses it, so what does the pitcher do? He throws another one. And usually, the hitter misses again. So something is learned from the point of view of the pitcher. Possibly the hitter as well.

Now, if the ball gets hit, then the pitcher knows he must change up his pitch when the hitter comes up to bat again. See, he didn't fail in having the batter hit the ball, he just learned what pitch not to throw next time.

Same thing with football. Each team creates a battle plan ahead of time depending on their strengths and weaknesses. They get out on the field and start to execute. If a play works, they try it again.

If a play doesn't, they try something else. That is why there is half-time. So each team can go back to the drawing board and revise their plan of action. You see this happen all the time in football. That is what makes it exciting to watch.

A team could be down in the first half and then come back to win in the second half. Remember the Super Bowl story?

When you have these types of failures in your time of creation or life in general, think of them as tests. A test to see if you have what it takes. A test to see if you are worthy of this change you are trying to create.

A chance to change your plan. That is what's great about America and why people risk their lives to get here. Because if you fail at anything you attempt, you can get up and try again. Again and again and again, until you get it right.

Like the old saying says, "if at first, you don't succeed, try, and try again." that is because there are lessons to be learned in failures and adversity. But in order to do this, you must have discipline and that burning desire for achievement.

I was driving down the street one day and I saw a big billboard sign, and on it was a picture of Abraham Lincoln. And in big letters, it said, "Failed, Failed, Failed, and then." Then in smaller letters underneath it said, "Persistence, pass it on."

Abraham Lincoln is a great example of learning from failure as he had many in his life. But through persistence, discipline, and a clear picture of what he wanted to create, he learned his lessons. Then what did he do?

Develop this mindset That way you can learn the lessons presented by failures that you will encounter.

Walt Disney was a success developed through failure. He had many hardships and setbacks to overcome on his journey as well. But he learned the lessons and created something that still lives on today. And not just lives, but thrives!

J.K. Rowling was practically homeless from the failures and setbacks she encountered in life. But she kept learning from her mistakes. She eventually got Harry Potter published and became a massive success.

Soichiro Honda is another great example of lessons learned from failure and adversity. For four decades he dealt with them and said that through them all he learned how to succeed and innovate his ideas.

And how about Steve Jobs getting fired from Apple? Can you imagine getting fired from your own company? After that happened he started again with new ideas. Next and Pixar. Then got back to Apple to become CEO.

So you see, it all comes down to how you deal with your failures and setbacks. Obstacles that life will throw at you, and adversities that you will run into. That is why you must have all the elements developed that are in this book.

If you do as instructed you will be able to create a whole new reality. Just learn from your mistakes along the way.

Chapter 9 Summary

In this chapter, you have learned about adversity. How there will be setbacks, roadblocks, and failures along your journey. And they will make you want to give up.

First, you learned that you can't give up because your desire to change is too great, and that there are lessons to be learned from your failures.

Second, you learned that this happens to every person who Persues success. Henry Ford and Thomas Edison both had many failures but learned their lessons.

Third, you learned how there are lessons learned from failure in sports. And it is the lessons learned from mistakes that make them so exciting to watch.

Fourth, you learned about how a few more people had to learn from their many failures. Walt Disney, J.K. Rowling, and Steve Jobs.

Fifth, you learned that you will need to be like all these people, to learn the lessons from your own failures. It will make a difference in you creating your new reality.

Learn from your failures and you will become unstoppable!

72

Chapter 10: Expectancy

Your order's been received

Another thing that all successful people do, is expecting their dreams to come true. They live a life of expectancy. They have put in their order to the universe, and expect that it is on its way. And you will learn to do the same.

This is very much like ordering a meal at a restaurant. You look over the menu, the waiter comes over to take your order, and you tell him/her what you want. They then write it down and go get it for you.

You then relax and don't worry about it. The reason why you can relax and not worry is that you expect that your order is being taken care of. And if it's not correct, you send it back until they get it right. Hopefully, they will the first time.

This is the way of the world we live in. Albert Einstein said that everything in the universe is made up of energy. Even us. And all energy vibrates at a specific frequency. All of us. We all vibrate at a certain frequency.

And the objective in creating our new reality is to match the frequency with that which we desire.

That is how you manifest things into your life. You get on the same frequency. Have you ever met someone and just automatically clicked with them? It is because you are both vibrating at the same frequency.

Same thing with someone you don't click with. You and they are vibrating at different frequencies. So your objective is to attract the people places and things needed for you to create your new reality.

And when you do as instructed, you will do that. So that is where expectancy comes in. If you have done all that I have taught you so far in this training, you can expect that you'll attract what you need to manifest your desires.

The reason for this is because of the scientific law behind it. If you expect it to happen with confidence, just like ordering at a restaurant, or online, you can expect it to manifest into your reality.

This means that you don't necessarily get what you want in life, but what you expect. If you expect to get success and you truly believe it to be so, there is no way that it will not develop in your life. It will.

But in order for it to do so, you must truly feel deep down inside that you are worthy of its expectancy.

Remember I taught you about adding feeling and emotion? Remember what I said about having faith and believing in yourself? Remember what I taught you about discipline? Well, all this will lead to you developing confidence.

Confidence that you have what it takes to create your new reality. And since everything vibrates and we all are mental transmitters, we are always sending and receiving signals. What we send out, comes back to us.

And by knowing this, you then can be assured that you will attract what you need, to get what you want out of life. And if you have taken control of your mind, you can expect it to happen. How long? That depends on you.

As a guitar teacher, I'm always asked, "how long will it take me to get good?', or "how many lessons will I need to learn the guitar?" And I always say, "it depends on you." This is the same thing. It all depends on your daily application.

It depends on how well you have studied the material. It depends on how much action you have taken on a daily basis. If you have done as instructed up to this point, you should have a different perspective on your future.

You should be confident that you can create the life you choose by taking control of your mind. If not, you need to study more.

If you have studied, written down, and done all that is instructed, you can expect that good things are happening now, and more is on its way. This is the law of the universe. This is the mental law that you are tapping into.

But like learning anything new, you need to follow the concepts and techniques involved and put them into practice on a daily basis in order for them to work. You can't just read and think, you have to also do what is necessary.

This is why most people fail to change their lives for the better. They may read some books, watch videos, and even think and write. But do they really believe it's possible? Do they put feeling into their vision?

No, they don't. Then they wonder why things didn't happen as the books or videos said they would. It's not the training that is the issue, it is the student learning, that is the issue. So think about this from your perspective.

If you are doing as instructed, you can expect that you will attract into your life what is needed to create the new reality you are looking to create. Like the goal, we mentioned earlier of doubling your income in the next twelve months.

Can it be done? Yes! That is if you are obsessed with doing everything necessary to make it happen.

Chapter 10 Summary

In this chapter, you have learned about having an attitude of expectancy. You must expect that all the training that you have been doing is going to bring about your desired outcome.

First, you learned that you are putting in an order to the universe very much like at a restaurant. And if you have done as instructed, except that it is on its way.

Second, you learned how we live in a world of vibrational frequency. And the objective is to match the frequency of that which you desire to be about your new reality.

Third, you learned that we are all mental transmitters that are always sending and receiving signals. And that you get back what you send out. Send out good, get back good.

Fourth, you learned that most people fail to make a positive change because they don't do all that is instructed. Then they feel this science does not work.

Fifth, you learned that it is not the science that is at fault, it is the student. And to make a positive change in your life, you must be willing to do daily whatever it takes to make it happen.

78

Chapter 11: Gratitude

Show appreciation

Once you have gotten to this point in the training, you should be feeling pretty good about all you have accomplished. All the things you have learned and know that the things you desire are on their way.

If not, then you need to go back and review some lessons. I hope that is not the case. I hope you are doing as instructed and seeing very clearly how this education has the potential to get you anything you want out of life.

If so, then you are now ready for our next lesson. Gratitude. This is where you show appreciation for what you currently have in life. This will open the river of abundance flowing in your direction.

You also want to show gratitude for what is on the horizon. The people, places, and things that are headed your way to produce what you desire in life. For it is gratitude that will help to make this happen.

Gratitude is a trait that all lasting successful people have. And they say it is what has helped them to accomplish their dreams.

Only in America can a person go from being broke to being a millionaire within a few years. And it is the power of gratitude that determines if they keep the money and improve their life, or if it slips through their finger and leaves them poor.

You see this happen all the time to people who get rich by all kinds of different means. Musicians have a hit and start making millions from it. Then they start spending it like its going out of style. Then it's time to write another hit.

When this doesn't happen, they get dropped from their label and they lose all their money. This happens because they were not grateful for the success that came their way. They took it for granted and in doing so, lost it all.

Athletes do this too. They make millions of dollars doing something they love to do, and gamble it all away. They get hurt, they get cut from the team, and they go broke. This happens because they didn't show gratitude.

Actors, make millions from movies. They buy big houses, fancy cars, etc. And if they don't show gratitude and appreciation, they end up losing their money too. You see it happen all the time.

People who win the lottery do the same thing. Some even end up worse off than before they won the lottery.

This happens because these people do not appreciate the good that has come to them through the work they do. They did not learn about money. They did not learn how to manage it. Or that it stays in the lives of those who do good with it.

Money is not bad or good. It is just a means of exchange for services rendered. It is what people do with it that gives it the reputation it has. Money has energy, and it flows to those who work for it.

And it stays in the lives of those who respect and appreciate its value. These are the people who built the country. The people who used it to help others. And this has been done through gratitude. And not just gratitude toward money, but gratitude towards all good in their lives.

This is something that you'll have to develop as well. Show the universe that you are grateful for what you have in your life right now. Even if it is only two pennies you can rub them together. This will help to get what you desi flowing in your direction.

Remember, I said to live like your new reality is here right now? Well, this is a great way to show gratitude. Being grateful will make you feel good about yourself. And in doing so, you will make those around you feel good.

Always be aware of how you feel about your life.

If you sit down once a week and write out what you are grateful for, and recite it with feeling, the universe will make sure that more good things come into your life. This will help you to create your new reality.

When people are not appreciative of what they have, they live a miserable life. I once worked with a guy like this. He made good money, even though he never graduated high school, but was never happy about it.

If you make good money, and you never graduated high school, let alone went to college, shouldn't you be grateful? After all, most people don't accomplish making good money without formal education.

Although the world is filled with successful people who never graduated high school. The difference between them and the person I'm talking about is gratitude. They had it and he didn't. That is why they felt good about life and he did not.

I could never understand that about him. He'd always complain that he didn't have money. Although he had his own home, multiple cars, and everything else anybody has. But yet when I talked to him, he didn't seem very happy.

He always complained that he didn't have any money, or that he wasn't making enough money.

What was interesting, is that he was in a leadership position. So he did make more money than most of the people who worked there. Yet he never felt grateful for what he had. That is why he lived such a miserable life.

After a while, I had to stay away from him because I thought it to be ridiculous. And like they say, "misery loves company." so since he was miserable, he wanted those around him to be miserable.

Make sure as you practice gratitude, that you stay away from these types of people. All they will do is bring you down. I believe that had this person I talk about been more grateful, he would have had more goodness flow into his life.

But since he wasn't, he cut off the flow of prosperity. As so many people in the world do. They don't appreciate what they have and in doing so, good passes them by and flows to those who do.

So it will be with you also. You start with where you are right now. You start with all that you have. Give thanks for all the things in your possession. All the technology has allowed you to live a better life.

When you are aware of what you have and don't focus on what you don't have, you will bring more goodness into your life.

Now, I realize knowing what you don't have is what propels you to move forward to get it. That makes sense. But you want to give attention to getting more while showing appreciation for what you already have. This is gratitude.

All successful people who have done well with what they have accomplished, have shown gratitude. That is why they have been able to keep their money and keep the river of prosperity flowing toward them.

Gratitude also magnifies your good spirit and promotes well-being. It can also lead to increased determination, enthusiasm, and academic achievement. Which is what this book is all about.

Being grateful will allow you to feel good about helping others in their time of need. That is why I've written this book and many others. To show gratitude for all the good that has been bestowed upon me.

When you are grateful, you also sleep better. This is because you feel better about yourself and what you have accomplished in life. Which will lead you to be determined to accomplish more. To be an inspiration to those around you.

Gratitude will open up a world of possibility to you.

Chapter 11 Summary

In this chapter, you have learned about the necessity of being grateful. Showing gratitude for what you have right now, as well as what you will be receiving in the near future.

<u>First</u>, you learned that all successful people who have everlasting success are grateful. They are grateful for what they have accomplished and that is why they stay successful.

<u>Second</u>, you learned about the types of people who don't show gratitude. And what happens to them when they are not grateful? Learn this lesson well.

<u>Third</u>, you learned how the river of prosperity continues to flow into the lives of those who show gratitude. The ones who are grateful and share their good fortune.

<u>Fourth</u>, you learned that although you are determined to gain more in life, you want to be aware of the good that is already in your life today. And not focus on what you don't have.

<u>Fifth</u>, you learned that gratitude can help with your well-being, and increased determination, and by being grateful, you can open a door to a whole new world of possibility.

86

Chapter 12: Let It Go

Give it time to manifest

Now that you have done all that is instructed, you want to let it go and give it time to manifest. Just like the farmer or baker. The farmer plants his seed and turns it over to the universe to make it happen.

Same thing with the baker. They put the bread in the oven, and let the universe do its thing. Sure you can watch the bread until it rises, but it's not going to rise any faster. Same thing here. Best to just have faith that it is well on its way.

That is if you did all that was instructed. If not, I'd highly recommend that you do so. The reason to just let go and let things happen is to let the universe know that you trust that it is being taken care of.

Remember what you learned about faith? Remember how I taught you how strong it needs to be? Well, here is a prime example of it. You must have faith in the process, the science that it is working.

And you should be taking daily action toward your new reality.

This is another reason why people fail to manifest what they desire. They get impatient. They let self-doubt creep in and take over their mental garden. They don't use their affirmations enough to make self-doubt go away.

Deep inside, they don't truly believe it's possible that they can create their new reality. These are the ones who are sitting on the couch waiting for something to happen. Not the ones who are out making something happen.

Now, it is important to sit, think, and meditate so that the subconscious mind can deliver you the plan needed. But once this happens, you must get going on putting that plan into action on a daily basis.

You won't see positive change without taking action on a daily basis. It is like learning to play the guitar. You can read the books, and watch the videos, but at some point, you are going to have to pick up the guitar.

Most successful people have such a burning desire for the change they are making, they are willing to work day and night for it. But at the same time, working toward the change without worrying that it will happen.

Same thing with learning the guitar. You have to trust, that if you do as instructed, you will one day be able to play it.

When you order food at a restaurant, you put in your order and wait for it to come to you when it is finished. You don't keep asking when it's going to come out, or if you should have ordered something else, or changed your mind.

You put in your order and then sit back, relax, and enjoy the company and surroundings knowing it is on its way. But for some reason, when it comes to manifesting through this science, people don't do that.

They get impatient. I know I have in the past. And I think it's only natural because we live in such an instant gratification world, we have a hard time waiting. We keep working toward the goal and negativity tries to creep in.

As you are working toward your goal, you will get those thoughts that creep in. Tell you things like "this isn't going to work." or when you make a mistake you'll hear things like "I told you so." and it will make you doubt yourself.

This is all-natural. Just make sure to stay steady with your purpose and faith and keep those affirmations handy. That way when negativity does pop up like a pesky weed, you can kill it right away.

As you take action, focus on the day, not the outcome, and all will be good in the end. Just stay steady with your faith.

When you get impatient, you cut off the natural flow of energy that is flowing to you. If you catch the attention of every shiny object, as a lot of people do, you change your mind about what you want.

This sends out mixed signals. Remember what I said about money, and how it has energy? Well if you get impatient, you disrupt the flow of it to you. Then like a river, it changes direction and starts flowing toward someone who isn't.

This is why having faith is so important. That's why having an expectancy is so important. Why having that initial purpose backed by a burning desire for its achievement is so important? Why showing gratitude is so important.

Do you think that you are showing gratitude to science and the universe when you are growing impatient? When you keep changing your mind about what you want? No. you are not. And in doing so, it holds up your order.

Just like at a restaurant. If you were to grow too impatient, they get irritated and hold your order. But if you relax, and let the chef cook the meal, then it is brought to you as requested. This is very true in sports as well.

In football, the receiver needs to have time to get downfield before the ball is thrown to him.

If the quarterback gets impatient or rushed by the linebacker, he throws the ball too early. Then the receiver doesn't catch the ball because he didn't give the play time to develop. Sometimes he doesn't have time to, but you get what I mean.

All good things come to those who wait. And for you, this is the same thing. Remember what you learned about the world we live in? That everything is made up of energy? And that you get back what you give out?

Well, if you stay focused on what you are giving out, the vibrational frequency you are seeking, you'll eventually find it. But you must be patient. Very much like tuning into a radio station.

Have you ever seen movies about robbers who try to crack a safe open? These guys have to have massive patience. To hear the tumblers turn as they are trying to find the right combination to open the safe.

They also have to have purpose backed by faith that if they work at it hard enough, they'll get it. They actually expect that they'll get it. That is why they are in that profession. You must be like that too with what you desire.

You must expect that it will manifest. When? You're not too sure, but you have purpose backed by faith that it one day will.

Chapter 12 Summary

In this chapter, you learned about the importance of relaxing and letting go. Keep working daily on your goal, but trust that the science works and it's on its way.

First, you learned that by letting go and having faith, you are letting the universe know that you are not worried. That you trust in the process.

Second, you learned that what you need to do most is just keep taking daily action. Focus on the work of the day and not the final outcome.

Third, you learned to beware of self-doubt that will try to creep in at any chance it gets. Especially when you are getting impatient. Be sure to have your affirmations ready.

Fourth, you learned that when you get impatient, you cut off the flow of energy toward what you desire to manifest. You need to keep this energy channel open and flowing freely.

Fifth, you learned that most people don't get results because they get impatient and lose faith. Don't do that. Keep steady with your purpose, backed by a burning desire.

Chapter 13: Master Alliance

Maximize your potential for success

Another thing successful people do is create a master alliance. A group of people that are all working together to accomplish the goal at hand. They find these people along their journey.

You too will want to do this. As you take daily action along your journey of making a change in your life for a better future, you will want to seek out those you can make allies with. People you feel can help you with completing your mission.

You always want to be on the lookout for these types of people. I recommend you write down on a sheet of paper, a list of who might be a good fit for your alliance group. Who might be in a position to help you?

This is a key principle in accomplishing your desires. As they say, "anyone can be successful, they just can't do it alone." And this is a very true statement. Even, though I teach by myself, I do have people who help me.

Like the people who run the studio, I rent. The mechanic helps me keep my vehicle running to get to class.

I also have people on the internet who help me with the guitar books that I publish, the online courses that I create, and my website. I could never do all this by myself. It is these people's knowledge that helps me do it.

The knowledge, expertise, and talents of others are what allow me to be a success along with my own. It is a group effort. That is really what success is all about. People work with people for the common good.

Now if you have a situation where you need to work face-to-face with a team of individuals, then you need to pick the right ones. The ones that will help you to create, grow, and expand your operation. Whatever it may be.

You want to pick people who have knowledge in areas that you don't. It is good to gain as much knowledge as you can for yourself, but sometimes there is not enough time in the day to gain it all. So you install someone who has.

Pick someone who has a specific kind of talent that will be beneficial to your mission. A talent that you don't possess. A talent that can save you time and money in the long run.

Pick people who have experience in areas that you don't. That experience can help you to gain insight into new ideas.

By working with these types of people, you learn to connect your mind with their abilities, foresight, and education. You might even need to use other people's money.

It's good to use your own money when you can, but some projects may be more than you can personally afford, so you may need to employ the money of other people. Like a bank. And that's ok, as long as you use it wisely.

You want to make sure that everyone is on the same page and that they are all working toward the same goal. To get you to where you are going, or help you to create your new reality. This is what the master alliance is all about.

You see this very clearly with big companies like Ford, Walmart, Home Depot, etc, etc, etc. They all have a team of people working together for the better of the good. Any type of real estate development works this way also.

Could Mcdonald's have a restaurant on just about every street corner in America without a master alliance? No, they couldn't. Could Walmart do the same? No, they couldn't. Any company that grows and expands, needs a master alliance.

I'm not sure what your new reality looks like, but you will need to create something of a sort as well to be successful.

You can choose to create any type of new reality you want. And if you don't have knowledge in a certain area, you can bridge it with someone else. You already do this, when you think about it.

You might not be creating a master alliance, but you already use the knowledge of someone else if you've ever hired a plumber or mechanic. Your master alliance is the same principle, you're just using them more frequently.

In my business of teaching guitar lessons, I don't need other teachers to teach for me, as I wouldn't want that anyway, but I do utilize other people's talents and expertise in other areas of my business. My master alliance.

For instance, my website. I developed it, but I need help to keep it maintained. So I use my hosting service to do that. They keep it operating at peak performance while I teach and they help me with suggestions to make it better.

I've had this website now for about 15 years. It has served me well. In fact, I just recently got selected as one of the top 12 guitar instructors in Denver for 2022. Not bad, being there are well over one hundred teachers in the metro area.

A lot of my being selected had to do with my website and the master alliance that helps me keep it running.

The same thing goes for my eBay store. I didn't develop the technology, wouldn't know how. But they do, and because of it, I am able to have a store and make money with it. And if I have any issues, my alliance is only a phone call away.

I just recently started building another store for my ebooks and courses. Once again, I don't know how to create the store platform, but my alliance does. They create the tools I need and I use them. When I make a sale, we all benefit.

If my vehicle has issues, I don't have the knowledge to fix it, or the time to learn, so I take it to my mechanic. He gets it fixed and I get back on the road to go teach. Making money from teaching allows me to pay him for his expertise.

The same thing goes for advertising on the internet. All advertising platforms help me to create my ads and track the performance of the ads. Surely I couldn't learn to do all this by myself. So I install the expertise of others.

Same thing with my book covers. I've learned to do them myself, but not without the expertise and knowledge of someone else. And, if there is a time in the future I don't have time to create them myself, I have a master alliance I can go to.

You will want to create this kind of alliance as well. People you can go to that will help you attain your personal success.

Chapter 13 Summary

In this final chapter, you learned about creating a master alliance. A group of people that help you to create your new reality with their talent, knowledge, and expertise.

First, you learned that it is best to write out a list on a sheet of paper of people who can help. This will get the gears in your mind moving in the right direction.

Second, you learned that you want individuals that have expertise and knowledge in areas that you don't. Areas that will be necessary to accomplish your mission.

Third, you learned that you will need this to grow and expand your operation. Depending on your new reality, will depend on how many. and what type of people you will need.

Fourth, you learned that all big companies, ones that you probably shop at from time to time, use master alliances. Places like Walmart, Home Depot, and Mcdonald's.

Fifth, you learned how I use a master alliance for my success. And that you can use these types of people as well for yours. You just need to figure out who you need and find them. As this will make a huge difference in your success.

Create A New Reality Conclusion

In this book, you learned 13 lessons needed to create your new reality. If you take each one, study it, and put it into practice, it will work. I know it will. That is why I am writing this book on the subject.

But in order for it to work, you must put all lessons into action on a daily basis. This is where a lot of people fail at creating their new life. They don't daily enough daily action. They don't do it because they don't have enough of a burning desire.

If your purpose is strong, and you have a burning desire for attaining the change you are looking for, you will then do what it takes to get the plan from your subconscious mind. You will then put this plan into action at once without question.

This is where faith comes in. If you don't fully believe in the science, and the fact that you can do it, then you won't take action enough to get it done. You might get started, but you won't stick with it until the end.

This is what successful people do. They hold their purpose in the front of their minds and develop a burning desire for its achievement. They receive the plan from their subconscious mind and put it into action on a daily basis.

They don't question, they just move forward. At the same time, they stay focused on additional assignments the mind sends them when it is needed. They know this is the process of achievement, so they do it without hesitation.

You will have to do the same. You will need to listen to your mind and when it presents you with ideas that cause you to step out of your comfort zone, you need to just do it. Don't ask why, just do it.

This is why the first lesson in this training that was taught was the lesson of thought. A change in anything starts with a thought. You think about making a change. You think about why you'd like to make a change.

You think about the possibility of change. That is really the only thing that you have control over in your life your thoughts. You don't have control of what is out in the world, but you do have control of your mind.

This is what separates the rich from the poor. The poor accept what life hands to them, whereas where the rich command what they want out of life. And this can only be done through having control of your thoughts.

The second lesson you learned was the importance of having a burning desire. Once you establish the thought of change, you need to develop a burning desire for its achievement. This is where a lot of people fail.

They fail because they don't have that fire burning in their belly. This is a must! All change in any area of life or the world has had this burning desire. You must have it too. You must truly want to make this change in order for it to happen.

As I mentioned to you why I'm writing this book and several of the others that I have authored. I wanted to make a change, had the desire to do so, and moved forward on learning what was needed to make it happen.

When I was chosen to teach, I went full steam ahead. I say chosen, because I didn't go to teaching, it chose me. The universe looked at my passion for playing guitar and my passion for change and decided to intervene.

The universe said, "Dwayne, you would make a great guitar teacher." so, I pursued that. Through books I read, I discovered the power of the subconscious mind and used it to make positive changes in my life.

And through having a burning desire, I did. You will need to do the same.

As I also mentioned, you'll want to write it down. Always write ideas that come to you down. I can't express the power of this technique enough. Writing things down and saying them out loud is how you communicate with your subconscious.

Remember, this part of your mind world 24/7 and is ready to help you make the change you desire. But you must learn how to communicate with it. And it starts with writing your ideas down and looking at them.

The third lesson you learned was that you must have a vision of your new reality. You must take some time to open the door to your imagination and use it to create the vision of your desired change.

Remember, all things in life were created twice. Once in the mind and once in reality. This is another step where writing will make a huge difference. In order for the subconscious mind to assist you, you must consciously give it specific orders.

This is done by visualizing to the point that you can write it out in specific detail. If you want a new car, what does it look like? What are the make and model? Color? Year? All this will help the mind to figure out how to help you get it.

Once you can clearly see that vision in specific detail, you then must begin to live as you have it right now. Today! I know this can be hard to do. But it is a must as well. It will help it to manifest into your new reality.

You must act as if. As if you already are living in a new home, driving a new car, working at a better job, etc. I remember reading a book by Brian Tracy and he was mentioning treating your job like you owned the company.

I did this, and it caused my mind to help me eventually form my own business. It helped me to eventually create my own products to sell. My own great service to help others. And this idea can help you as well.

But in order for it to work, you must have a vision, backed by a burning desire for it to manifest in your life. These two things will build on themselves and take you far in life. But your vision must be clear and unwavering.

Think of all the great things created throughout the world. They all had two things in common. They all required vision, and they all required money. The new reality that you hope to create will require these two things as well.

Be sure to keep this in mind as you head down the road of creating your new reality with vision and desire.

We now come to your fourth lesson learned, adding feeling and emotion to your vision. This is very important because, without it, the body will not take enough action on a daily basis to make this change you desire a reality.

You can have the vision, but if you don't add emotion and feeling to it, you won't be able to act it out as I mentioned. This acting out is a way to communicate with the mind as well as get on the right vibrational frequency.

Remember, I taught you about everything being energy, and all energy vibrates? Well here is where this comes in to create your new reality. You learn to get on the same vibrational frequency as that which you desire.

Everything vibrates at a certain frequency. Very much like a guitar. The strings of a guitar all need to vibrate at the same frequency for the instrument to sound good when you play it. If a string is on another frequency, it doesn't sound right.

It then needs to be tuned to the correct frequency. Once it does then it sounds good. What you desire is very much like that. You need to get in harmony with the frequency that matches what you want in life.

As Einstein said, "match the frequency and there is no way that you cannot have that which you desire."

The next lesson learned was the importance of having faith. Faith in the process, and faith in yourself. If you don't truly believe that the process works, it won't. Certain actions will cause certain reactions, as this is science.

But without faith, it won't happen like you'd like it to. You must believe that if you do as instructed, you will create your new reality. I know it to be true because it has worked for me. But you must believe it to be true for it to work for you.

Not only do you need to believe in the process, but you need to also have faith in yourself that you can step out of your comfort zone and do what it takes to make it happen. Remember, the lesson on deciding what you are willing to give?

Nothing is free in this world. You must deliver as good as you wish to receive. And in order for you to do this, you need to have faith. Do you want a million dollars? You must provide a million dollars worth of products or services.

In order for anyone in any industry to do that, they must have faith in themselves that they can. If you have faith in yourself that you can, then you will. But you must believe in the possibility.

Through the power of belief and faith, there is nothing that you can't bend to your will. So, develop faith.

If you need help in this area, just look to the great life changers of the world. People like Henry Ford, Steve Jobs, Jimi Hendrix, J.K. Rowling, and Abraham Lincoln. All of these people did succeed in their chosen fields due to faith.

Your faith will also help guard against opposing people who will tell you it can't be done. Or your own individual thoughts that will try to creep in like unwanted weeds and pests. Faith will help you to banish them.

This is why it is also best to keep your thoughts and desires to yourself. Believe me, when you make the great change that you are shooting for, you will have plenty to talk about. Then you can pay it forward by showing others how you did it.

Remember, you are a mental gardener and you must protect your garden. Your dream garden. You must plant the seeds, nourish them and nurture them when they start to develop. Faith will help you to do this.

Just like a gardener, or baker, you must trust in the process and have faith that the universe is not going to let you down. That if you do your job, it will be glad to do its job. You both will be working in harmony.

Once you firmly have your desire, vision, and faith established, it is time to develop a strategy. A plan for your new reality's attainment. This is where you'll give in order to get comes in. Where you will step out of your comfort zone.

That's right, step out of your comfort zone. It is the only way to do it. Remember what I told you about me going to strangers' homes and trying to convince them that I knew what I was doing? That my friend was scary.

As I mentioned before, the cave you fear entering holds the treasure you seek. Remember this is like a mantra. Because it is so true. So make sure that your strategy has you doing things you don't normally do.

This is how growth is done and your strategy must incorporate this in order for it to be effective. This is another reason why a lot of people don't make changes. They don't want to step out of their comfort zone.

Listen to your subconscious mind, it will guide you as to what to do. When it gives you an idea, write it down. Take action on it. Once you have your strategy mapped out, start advancing forward. Your new reality is just over the horizon.

The next lesson on the list is discipline. In order for you to make all the lessons work in harmony with each other, you must have discipline. The road to personal success for anyone is a rocky one. It is not smoothly paved with asphalt.

It is a very rocky unproven road. A road is full of uncertainties. This is why faith is so important o have, this is why desire is so important to have, and this is why having discipline is so important to have also.

Here is another lesson that people fail at. They don't have the discipline to see it through. Remember, the change that you are wanting to make is the destination of a journey that you are going to take. And you must have the discipline to do it.

It is very much like learning to play the guitar. You must have the discipline to see it through. It won't come overnight. Some concepts and techniques might be, but putting them all together to create music will take some time and discipline.

That is why most people fail to learn the guitar, and why most people fail at any type of change they wish to produce. They don't have the discipline to see it through to the end. You must have this discipline.

You must be willing to do whatever it takes. Even at times when you don't feel like it. That is discipline.

Affirmations are the next lesson you want to master. These are your negative thought killers. These are the statements that you communicate with your subconscious mind. These are what keep you going in rough weather.

These are what keep you from worrying about things, these are what keep out self-doubt. And believe me, self-doubt will try to creep in at any chance it gets. Just like cold weather in the winter. Affirmations help keep this out.

Affirmations are like the forcefield in Star Wars that the rebels have to put up to keep out the Empire. Affirmations are your weed killer and pest control for your mental garden. These are what will keep you in a positive state of mind.

Remember, learning about being successful is a state of mind. You see this in sports all the time. They give themselves pep talks to affirm that they are going to win the game. Affirmations are a huge part of success.

They are also what help to program your subconscious mind to assist you in accomplishing your desires. Remember, your mind is like a stubborn child that doesn't want to change. But will, if you take repeated action upon it daily.

You must tell it what you want it to do repeatedly over and over again for it to conform. And affirmations are how you do it.

The next lesson that needs to be learned is a hard one. Probably the hardest of them all. The lesson of learning from adversity. Learning from failure. This is part of life. We all fail. Even the most successful people.

The difference is, that successful people look for the lesson inside the adversity. They don't look at something that didn't work out as a failure. They don't look at adversity as a roadblock.

They look at it as a chance to learn something new. They look at it as a chance to change their plans. A chance to start over again. A chance to look at things from a new angle. A better way to do old things from a new perspective.

Remember what you learned about Thomas Edison? How it took him over ten thousand times to invent the light bulb? And when asked if he had failed, he said, "no, I just figured out another way of how not to do it."

You must have this kind of attitude as well. When something doesn't work out, be happy to go back to the drawing board and try again. Design a new plan, Try an old idea in a new way, etc. But most of all, stay positive through the process.

I know this can be hard. But it is necessary. It is what will separate you from the rest of the crowd.

You then learn the lesson of expectancy. Successful people from all walks of life expect success. That is why Thomas Edison was willing to keep trying after so many attempts at inventing the light bulb.

He expected that he's figured it out. You must do the same. You must expect that the new reality that you are trying to create is on its way. And this will be apparent because you are acting like it is in your life right now.

Just like shopping online and putting in your order. You expect it to be delivered. And it usually is. Sometimes there is an issue with the delivery, but for the most part, it is delivered. Once you put in your order you expect it to be delivered.

This is the same way. You put in your order to the universe and expect that it has been received and that it will be delivered. Don't worry about it. This is the way to success. You must expect it to happen. This is also where faith comes in.

Remember also, that your mind is a transmitter that is always sending and receiving signals. And the thoughts you send out, come back to you in a physical equivalent. So, send out the right thoughts, and expect them to come back to you.

Just make sure you are crystal clear about what you want, or your order might not come out correctly.

The next lesson to learn is a very important one as well. The lesson of gratitude. You must show gratitude for what you want and be grateful for what you have right now. All successful people mention the importance of this.

The reason why this is so important is that it opens the floodgates of prosperity flowing in your direction. This is what you are going to need if you plan on making any type of lasting change in your life.

When you can be grateful for what you have right now, even if it's not much, you develop a better attitude. Having a good positive attitude can make a world of difference. And showing gratitude will help develop this.

Being grateful has also been known to help with well-being. When you feel good, you approach life from a better perspective. You have increased determination, better focus, and motivation to succeed.

Gratitude is also what is going to help you get up when life has knocked you down. As this will happen from time to time. Being grateful for the good that is in your life and what's on it's way will help you to get up and press on.

Remember, you are on a journey to making positive changes in your life. And gratitude will be a tool that will serve you well.

Now once you have done all that is instructed, you then have to let it go. Relax and know that the universe has received your order. This is where a lot of people who try to make change fail. They get too anxious for things to happen right now.

This is to be expected because we live in an instant-gratification world. Unfortunately, it takes a bit to get your order delivered to you. Just like at a restaurant, you must give it time. The same thing goes with the gardener or baker.

If you put water in a pan and set it at a certain degree of heat, it will eventually boil. But, it is not going to boil sooner by you watching it. This goes with bread rising. Watching the oven is not going to make it rise quicker.

Same thing with planting a seed in the ground. It takes a certain amount of time for it to germinate. Then you have to give it time to grow into what you want to harvest. Your new reality works the same way.

You just need to relax, keep advancing forward in taking daily action and all will work out in the end. This is where faith comes in again. See how important faith is to the process? You need not worry or be impatient.

If you keep doing all that has been instructed, you will come out ahead.

And last but not least, build yourself a master alliance. A group of individuals that can help you in all areas of your life. Even if you don't work with the all at once, you'll need to be able to turn to others for their expertise.

Remember what I told you about my alliance? I don't work with a group of people face to face, but I do have a group of people that I do rely on for their skillsets and knowledge. Even this book that I'm writing, needs other people's expertise.

You will need to find people as well for the things that you are working on. For what you are trying to accomplish. You will need to make contacts, and as you do, you will progress forward on the new reality you are working at making.

Especially if you want to have a big company full of employees and managers. They will become your master alliance. People you learn to depend on. So make sure you don't overlook this. Because you can't be successful alone.

Do all this on a daily basis and you will see the results you are looking for. You might even discover some great things about yourself. And most of all have fun along your journey.

Best of luck, study, and have fun
Sincerely, Dwayne Jenkins
Tritone Publishing. copyright © 2023

About the Author

Dwayne Jenkins is a self-accomplished musician and a professional guitar teacher. Along with a student of the science of success. He has been learning, playing, and teaching guitar lessons throughout Denver, CO for almost two decades.

Through the teachings in this book was able to build a very successful guitar-teaching business, and create the reality that he wanted. As you can do this as well.

Dwayne has run this business for almost twenty years with much success in this arena. He has also authored books on how to play guitar that has sold to students around the world.

Along with authoring guitar books, Dwayne is currently writing books on how to become successful. Not in just teaching guitar, but becoming successful at that which you desire. Anything you choose in life can be yours.

So if you're a student looking to start, or a student looking to further your education, be sure to get involved with Dwayne Jenkins and learn what so many people have already learned.

That the science of success is possible for you too.